D0065516

SandCastle

Do Something About It!

Do Something in Your Community

Amanda Rondeau

Consulting Editor, Diane Craig, M.A./Reading Specialist

Published by ABDO Publishing Company, 4940 Viking Drive, Edina, Minnesota 55435.

Printed in the United States.

Credits
Edited by: Pam Price
Curriculum Coordinator: Nancy Tuminelly
Cover and Interior Design and Production: Mighty Media
Photo Credits: BananaStock Ltd., Corbis Images, Comstock, Eyewire Images, Rubberball Productions, Skjold Photography

Library of Congress Cataloging-in-Publication Data

Rondeau, Amanda, 1974-.
   Do something in your community / Amanda Rondeau.
   p. cm.--(Do something about it!)
   Includes index.
   ISBN 1-59197-572-7
   1. Child volunteers--Juvenile literature. 2. Social action--Juvenile literature. 3. Community development--Juvenile literature. 4. Quality of life--Juvenile literature. I. Title. II. Series.

   HQ784.V64 R663 2004
   361--dc21
                                                    2003058392

SandCastle™ books are created by a professional team of educators, reading specialists, and content developers around five essential components that include phonemic awareness, phonics, vocabulary, text comprehension, and fluency. All books are written, reviewed, and leveled for guided reading, early intervention reading, and Accelerated Reader® programs and designed for use in shared, guided, and independent reading and writing activities to support a balanced approach to literacy instruction.

Let Us Know

After reading the book, SandCastle would like you to tell us your stories about reading. What is your favorite page? Was there something hard that you needed help with? Share the ups and downs of learning to read. We want to hear from you! To get posted on the ABDO Publishing Company Web site, send us e-mail at:

sandcastle@abdopub.com

SandCastle Level: Transitional

You can make a difference in your community by doing something to make it a better place to live.

When you do something to help others, you are making a difference.

Dr. Thomas and
Dr. Ortega want to help
sick people.

That is why they became
doctors.

Mr. Peters wants to help the kids in his community get better grades.

He tutors students after school.

Ms. Ritter wants kids to love sports as much as she does.

She coaches a lacrosse team in the summer.

Mr. Casas wants to help people in his community.

He became a firefighter.

Sarah, Chris, and Gary know their neighbor is sick and can't rake her leaves.

They are going to rake them for her.

Marty and Kim want to make their neighborhood a safe place to live.

They get to know the other families in their neighborhood.

Maria wants to help
people who don't have
enough food.

She serves meals at a
soup kitchen.

Nicole and her mom plant a community garden.

They donate the food they grow to people who are hungry.

There are many ways you can make a difference in your community.

What would you like to do?

Glossary

art. works such as paintings, sculptures, dances, and music created by arranging color, shape, motion, or sound

community. any group of people living in the same area or having common interests

doctor. someone whose job it is to help people who are sick or hurt

donate. to give a gift to charity

firefighter. someone whose job it is to put out fires

garden. a place where flowers, vegetables, or other plants are grown

lacrosse. a team sport in which the players each use a stick with a net on the end to carry, throw, and catch the ball while trying to score goals

neighbor. someone who lives near you

neighborhood. the people and houses in a particular area

rake. to gather together or to smooth out

soup kitchen. a place that serves free food, usually soup and bread, to people in need

sport. a physical activity done for fun, either alone or as part of a team

About SandCastle™

A professional team of educators, reading specialists, and content developers created the SandCastle™ series to support young readers as they develop reading skills and strategies and increase their general knowledge. The SandCastle™ series has four levels that correspond to early literacy development in young children. The levels are provided to help teachers and parents select the appropriate books for young readers.

Emerging Readers
(no flags)

Beginning Readers
(1 flag)

Transitional Readers
(2 flags)

Fluent Readers
(3 flags)

These levels are meant only as a guide. All levels are subject to change.

ABDO
Publishing Company

To see a complete list of SandCastle™ books and other nonfiction titles from ABDO Publishing Company, visit **www.abdopub.com** or contact us at:

4940 Viking Drive, Edina, Minnesota 55435 • 1-800-800-1312 • fax: 1-952-831-1632

MAR · 2005

**Indianapolis
Marion County
Public Library**

Renew by Phone
269-5222

Renew on the Web
www.imcpl.org

For general Library information
please call 269-1700.